Opening Devotions for Women's Groups

Deborah Edwards

BAKER BOOK HOUSE
Grand Rapids, Michigan 49506

Copyright 1985 by
Baker Book House Company

ISBN: 0-8010-3428-0

Printed in the United States of America

Contents

Preface

This book will be many things to many people. For some, it will be a call to worship, for others, a meditation. For me, it has been a journey.

Individual selections from this book can be used as a brief devotional to open a meeting or read as part of a worship service. The text for each piece appears at the top of the page and should be read first. Every piece is built upon the sure foundation of the Word and so will yield, in its few short lines, a blessing from the Lord.

Beyond its use in corporate worship, I trust this book will be used of the Lord as a guide for personal meditation. These pieces were not written as poetry, but they contain many poetic elements. One aspect of this may be seen in the placement of the words on the page. The short lines are designed to help the reader focus on individual ideas and images, to see the movement, the flow of a concept as it approaches its conclusion. This visual communication can be enjoyed only by the reader, although I hope it might be conveyed in some sense to a listener.

May I suggest to anyone using this book for personal devotions that you first read the text at the top of the page, then read the piece which follows. At the bottom of the page, you will find a list of additional references which were used in the writing of the piece. Look up each Scripture reference to see the context from which the Lord's message has come. Then reread the piece, asking the Lord to apply his truth to your heart. Make the words your prayer, the beginning of your conversation with the Lord on that topic.

It may help you to know, as you read through the book, that you are reading an account of a journey. This journey of trust, of abiding in him, began for me about a year ago and is detailed in another book, *The Songs of Deborah*. Recently the Lord led me to begin to write *Opening Devotions for Women's Groups*. Each morning I met with the Lord, studied his Word, and through his direction, wrote a piece. You will find them here in the order in which they were written.

Walk with me, then, through times of difficulty and testing. See the path leading through temptation and on to triumph in the Lord who is our Rock and our Salvation. Sing a new song to the Shepherd who cares for us so tenderly. Bow down in worship to the eternal King whose splendor and majesty is beyond our understanding. Glorify the Lord with me for all he is, and for all he is doing on our behalf.

Consider thoughtfully the road before us. The Lord has revealed himself to us in his Word for a purpose. He has shown himself to me in the writing of this book, and I believe that you, too, will see him in these pages. To what end? That we may glorify the Lord, that we may be his presence to all around us. He is calling us to be his love, his peace, his joy, his hope to a desperate, dying world. But before we can be his presence for others, we need to see the Lord as he really is. Then we can be a reflection of his light; we can radiate his love to all around.

Let us continue the journey then. Let us go on in him.

Part 1

In Him I Live
and Have My Being

A righteous man may have many troubles,
but the LORD delivers him from them all. [Ps. 34:19]

Promises

No one ever said
It would be easy—
Certainly not you, Lord.
You never said
There wouldn't be
Difficulties,
But you promised
To be my refuge
In times of trouble.
You never said
I wouldn't be
Surrounded
By frightening circumstances,
But you promised
To deliver me

From all my fears.
You never said
I wouldn't be
Brokenhearted,
But you promised
To save me
Even when I was
Crushed in spirit.
I would have asked
For the easy road, Lord,
But instead
You have given me,
In all my troubles,
The sure promise of
Deliverance.

Ps. 34:17–19

I will extol the LORD at all times;
his praise will always be on my lips. [Ps. 34:1]

Always

O Lord, let there
Always be
Praise on my lips
For you.
Not just in the easy times
When things are going well,
But in my affliction, Lord,
In my deepest distress,
Let my soul rejoice
In you.
O Lord, let me
Always bring
Glory to your name,
Not just in the public places
Where I am sometimes
   tempted
To share the glory

But in the quiet, private
   moments.
In the most intimate dealings,
Let my life honor
Only you.
O Lord, let me
Always look
To you.
Let my face shine
With the pleasure
Of knowing you.
Let my life radiate
Your beauty,
Your love,
Your goodness,
Not just some of the time, but
Always.

Ps. 34:1–3, 5

Taste and see that the LORD is good;
blessed is the man who takes refuge in him. . . .
those who seek the LORD lack no good thing. [Ps. 34:8, 10b]

Goodness

My good ideas,
My good intentions
Can lead me astray, Lord,
If I rely on them instead of
Relying on you.
When I seek my own way,
However appealing
It may seem,
I end up with the taste
Of ashes in my mouth.
Teach me to seek only you,
Lord.
Then I will lack nothing
That is good.
When I depend on my strength,
However tempting it may seem,
I end up with the

Bitter realization of
My own weakness.
Teach me to take refuge
In you, Lord.
Then I will taste and see
That you are good.
Teach me to delight
myself
In you, Lord.
Fill all my senses with
The taste, the sight,
The sound, the scent,
The touch
Of you.
Fill me with yourself,
That I may rejoice
In your goodness.

Ps. 37:4

I seek you with all my heart;
  do not let me stray from your commands. [Ps. 119:10]

Wholeheartedly

I seek you now, O Lord,
With all my heart.
This is something new for me.
I am far more used to
Halfheartedly seeking you
In times of need,
Not in times of abundance;
In times of fear,
Not in times of security.
I was unwilling, Lord,
To come to you with
All myself,
At all times.
Oh, I came readily
With a broken heart,
Asking you to do

For me.
But I came slowly
With an open heart,
Willing to do
For you.
Now, finally, you have so
Overwhelmed me with
Your unfailing love,
I can only come
To you with a heart
Filled with the desire
To know you,
To love you,
To do your will.
I praise you, Lord,
Wholeheartedly.

Ps. 119:2–5

I run in the path of your commands,
    for you have set my heart free. [Ps. 119:32]

Freedom

Freedom versus obedience:
It always seemed
This was the choice.
I could be free to choose
My own way, or
I could obey you, Lord.
I rebelled endlessly
Against your will
Because it left me
No option
But obedience—
I thought that meant
An end
To personal freedom.
But now you have
Opened my eyes to the

Wonderful peace
Of following
Your precepts.
You have taught me
To delight
In the path of
Your commands.
You have given me
The desire to choose
The way of truth, and
The will to set my heart
On your law.
Through obedience
To you, O Lord,
I have at last
Been made free.

Ps. 119:33–35

13

The LORD is compassionate and gracious,
    slow to anger, abounding in love.
He does not treat us as our sins deserve
    or repay us according to our iniquities. [Ps. 103:8, 10]

Compassion

How tenderly
You deal with me,
How willing you are
To forgive. Though
I come to you
Time after time
With the same old sins,
A reflection of my
Imperfect love toward
    you,
Still
You repay me with
Perfect love,
Graciously extended as
Infinite forgiveness.
As my Father-Creator,

You know my frailty,
You know my limitations.
But there is no limit
To your great
Love for me,
Your little child whom
You have called
To obedience.
I praise you, O Lord,
With all that I am,
For you have
Forgiven my sins,
Redeemed my life, and
Crowned me with your
Everlasting love and
Compassion.

Ps. 103:2–4, 8–14, 17–18

Unless the LORD builds the house,
   its builders labor in vain. [Ps. 127:1]

Vanity

The deception is
To believe I can do it
All myself,
To believe in
My own capability,
My own strength.
The temptation is
To forget that
Without you,
I can toil and try
From morning to night,
And then find my efforts
All in vain.
The truth is simply this:
All my strength is

Foolishness
When I rely
On it, instead of
Depending on your
Mighty power. You,
O Lord, and only you,
Are my strength.
I can rest in your
Strong arms and know
You will carry me along
In your perfect will,
And all that is
   accomplished
Will be done in truth,
Never in vain.

Ps. 127:1–2

God is our refuge and strength,
    an ever present help in trouble.
Therefore we will not fear . . . . [Ps. 46:1–2a]

Refuge

Where can I go
When my world falls
Down around me?
Where can I stand
When the earth gives way
Beneath my feet?
How can I endure
The overwhelming distress
Which threatens to
Engulf me?
O Lord, there is no place
For me to go,
No way for me to stand.
I cannot endure
Apart from your strength.
You are the Lord,

Mighty in power.
Your presence is
My constant
Assurance of help
In time of trouble.
I need not fear,
For you are at work
Through all circumstances,
To the glory of your name.
I need only
To be still,
Be still
And know
That you are God,
My strength and
My refuge.

Ps. 46:1–3, 10–11

16

> Do not fret because of evil men
>   or be envious of those who do wrong . . . .
> Refrain from anger and . . .
>   do not fret—it leads only to evil. [Ps. 37:1, 8]

Release

When I look to others
Who have chosen
The broad path of
Self-indulgence,
And see them
    enjoying
What appears to be
Success,
I can so easily fall
Into the fretful snare
Of envy.
I can twist and turn
In my jealous anger,
Caught in an
Evil trap.
But when I look

To you, Lord,
Your word comes
Quietly: "Be still;
Wait patiently.
Trust in me,
For I am the Lord."
Such sweet release
Comes then, Lord.
Peace replaces the
Worrisome bonds,
And I am free
To enjoy your
Abundant provision
To the faithful,
A lasting
Inheritance.

Ps. 37:7–9, 11, 16–18

Delight yourself in the LORD
and he will give you the desires of your heart. [Ps. 37:4]

Delight

Trust comes first.
Without complete trust
In you, Lord,
I am unwilling to accept
The place you have
Chosen for me.
I am unable to enjoy
The quiet rest of your
Safekeeping.
But with trust in you
Comes delight,
The pure delight of
   knowing
I am loved,
I am cared for by the
Shepherd of my soul.

You, Lord, provide all
My heart's desires
When my pleasure is
In you.
And as I trust,
As I delight myself
In your care,
I find my one desire—
To commit my way
To you, Lord,
Without reservation.
May all my days
Shine like the dawn,
A reflection of
Your presence,
My Delight.

Ps. 37:3–6

The LORD is my light and my salvation—
whom shall I fear?
The LORD is the stronghold of my life—
of whom shall I be afraid? [Ps. 27:1]

Safekeeping

The one desire
Of my heart
Is to know you, Lord.
I seek your face,
The intimate knowledge
Of who you are.
I seek the place
Of your dwelling,
The shelter of the
Rock, my Salvation.
In your presence is
No shadow of fear.
The light of your
     beauty
Fills my vision.
From the high place of

Your stronghold I see,
With new perspective,
The troubles which
Besiege me,
And I am unafraid.
For though I am
Surrounded
By that which would
Cause me to stumble
And fall, still
My confidence
Is in the Lord.
My song
Is one of joy;
My life, in your
Safekeeping.

Ps. 27:4–6

He reached down from on high and took hold of me;
  he drew me out of deep waters.
He rescued me from my powerful enemy,
  from my foes, who were too strong for me. [Ps. 18:16–17]

Rescue

When I wander
From the refuge
And seek my own way,
How easily
I become entangled with the
Cares and concerns of life—
The coils of worry
Are a ready snare.
Caught helpless in this trap,
I am overwhelmed by the
  flood,
A rising tide of faithless fear,
A foe too strong
For me. Then, from the
Depths of my distress
I call to you, the Lord,
My deliverance. Always

You hear my cry.
Always you come to me
In power and majesty,
And mercifully, you
Reach down, take hold,
  and
Lift me out of
Deep and fearful waters.
I cannot save myself from
The cold power of dread,
But you, O Lord, are
My salvation,
And worthy of praise,
For you rescue me,
And I am restored
To the stronghold
Of trust.

Ps. 18:4, 6, 16–19

It is God who arms me with strength
and makes my way perfect. [Ps. 18:32]

Victory

Against the enemy,
Against the temptations
Which surround me,
I am helpless.
My weakness
Always leads me on
The downward path
Of defeat.
But you, Lord,
With grace and mercy,
Stoop low to lift me
From my destructive course.
You set my feet
In your perfect way,
You strengthen my purpose
So I will not turn from it.

You arm me for the battle
With your shield of victory,
And knowing my need,
With your right hand
You hold the shield
Before me.
With your help, Lord,
I can advance against the
Barricade of difficulties
Which tempt me to despair.
I can scale any wall,
I can stand on the heights,
For you, O Lord,
Arm me with strength.
In your way
Is victory.

Ps. 18:29–36

The Lord lives! Praise be to my Rock!
Exalted be God my Savior! [Ps. 18:46]

Praise

I will sing praises
To you, Lord.
I will sing praises
To your name.
You are my Rock!
In you I have found
Refuge, a sure fortress
When strong temptation
Besieges me.
You are my Savior!
In you I have found
Deliverance, a way of escape
When my enemy
Pursues me.
It is you, O Lord, who
Subdues the tempter.

It is you who
Saves me from my enemy.
You have rescued me
From my powerful foe.
You have exalted me
In great victory,
Victory won
In the strength of
Your right hand,
Your hand which sustains me
With unfailing kindness.
For though I falter,
You will never fail.
You are the Lord!
Let all who hear the Name
Praise the Lord.

Ps. 18:1–3, 46–50

The heavens declare the glory of God;
    the skies proclaim the work of his hands. [Ps. 19:1]

Proclaim

Since the creation
Of the world, you
Have revealed yourself
To all men.
Your eternal power,
Your divine nature
Have been clearly seen.
You have placed,
As one witness
To all the earth,
The delicate canopy
Of the heavens.
Across this pavilion
The sun makes its circuit,
Day after day proclaiming
Your unfailing mercy.

Under the pitched tent
Of darkness, we see
The night sky, strewn
With a path of stars,
Night after night declaring
Your vast knowledge.
O Lord, let my voice blend
With the voice of the heavens,
Let me join with all
Creation as witness to
Your glory.
The stars are eloquent
In their silence.
Give me tongue to tell,
To proclaim to all
The glory of God.

Rom. 1:19–20

Precious

O Lord,
As your beloved,
I find true delight
In obeying
Your will. Your expressed
Purpose for me
Is perfect in every way.
I cherish your commands,
For they are given by one
Who is worthy
Of my trust.
As I learn to love
Your law,
You revive my spirit,
You make me wise,
You give light
To my eyes, and joy
To my heart.
The way you have ordained
For me is altogether
Right. Like the sweet
Taste of honey
Is the satisfaction of
Pleasing you.
O Lord, you have given me
A gift most precious,
Your revealed will.
May I treasure
Your word.
May my pleasure
Be in serving you,
And my reward as well.

Ps. 19:7–11

Keep your servant also from willful sins;
   may they not rule over me.
Then will I be blameless,
   innocent of great transgression. [Ps. 19:13]

Blameless

Lord, I cannot know
The iniquity of my heart,
For my heart is
Deceitful, hiding from me
The extent of my
Transgression.
Apart from your mercy,
I was enslaved by
The deadly lie
Of sin.
But you have set me
Free from sin—
All praise be to you!
You have made me
A servant of righteousness,
A servant of the most high

God, the Redeemer
Of my soul.
You keep me now
From willful sin—
As I submit to
Your rule,
I am free
Of wrongdoing.
You have taken this
Rebel heart
And, by grace alone,
Declared it innocent.
You have made me
Holy unto you,
And in your sight,
Blameless.

Rom. 6:22; Ps. 19:12–13

> Then I acknowledged my sin to you
>   and did not cover up my iniquity.
> I said, "I will confess
>   my transgressions to the LORD"—
> and you forgave
>   the guilt of my sin. [Ps. 32:5]

Confession

The ill effects of sin
Are a poison
To my soul.
When I choose the way
Of wrongdoing,
I am infected with
The toxin of deceit.
As I try to hide
My sin in the silence
Of the night,
My strength is
Undermined.
Through the day
My joy in you
Wastes away
Until I am left
With nothing.
But when I acknowledge
My sin
To you, and
Do not cover up
My iniquity,
You forgive me
Graciously, O Lord.
You purge from me
The taint of guilt.
You purify me
From all unrighteousness.
How foolish is the attempt
To conceal my transgression.
May I come to you quickly
With my confession.

Ps. 32:3–5; 1 John 1:9

Blessed is he
whose transgressions are forgiven,
whose sins are covered. [Ps. 32:1]

Covered

I thank you, O Lord,
For you have forgiven
My iniquity. My sins
You have covered.
You do not count
Against me my many
Transgressions.
You have credited to me
Righteousness in the
  name
Of my Redeemer.
You have blessed me
With your love
And grace.
Now let me be a
Blessing to others. To

Your dearly loved children,
Let me show compassion
Even when they
Are unkind.
Let me be gentle
In the face of
Their impatience.
With true humility,
Let me bear with them
And forgive them
Even as you, Lord,
Have forgiven me—
Graciously, and in love.
For it is with love that
A multitude of sins
Is covered.

Ps. 32:1–2; Rom. 4:5–8; Col. 3:12–14; 1 Peter 4:8

> I will instruct you and teach you in the way you should go;
> I will counsel you and watch over you. [Ps. 32:8]

Counsel

O Lord, you have
Promised to those
Who love you and
Obey you
A Comforter to
Lead them into
All truth.
I thank you, Lord,
For this illuminating
Gift, for by
Your Spirit of truth
I am instructed.
It is the holy Teacher
Who brings to my mind
Your Word, the guide
Which shows me
The way to go.
As I follow in submission
To your will,
Trusting that the path
You have shown me
Is perfect and right,
You provide for me
Peace—the absence of fear.
My comfort is in
Your love, which never fails.
My confidence is in
The Lord,
My joy in his
Good counsel.

Ps. 32:8–10; John 14:15–17a, 26–27

All you have made will praise you, O LORD;
   your saints will extol you.
They will celebrate your abundant goodness
   and joyfully sing of your righteousness. [Ps. 145:10, 7]

Celebration

Great is our God, the
Eternal King!
Through all the generations
His name will be
Praised. For ever and ever,
The most worthy
Name of the Lord
Will be praised!
All he has made
Will praise him;
His saints will extol
The mighty acts
Of his hand.
They will tell of
The awesome power
Of his works.

They will proclaim
The glorious splendor
Of his kingdom,
So all men may
Know the might and
The majesty of
The Lord
Whose kingdom is
Everlasting. My Lord,
Every day may I
Praise you with joy-filled
Song. As long as I live,
May my spirit rejoice with
Unending jubilation. May I
Magnify your name, O Lord,
In constant celebration.

Ps. 145:1–13a

The LORD is faithful to all his promises
   and loving toward all he has made.
The LORD is near to all who call on him,
   to all who call on him in truth. [Ps. 145:13b, 18]

Loving

O Lord, we cannot know
The depths
Of your majestic greatness,
But oh!
The limitless expanse
Of your unfailing love—
You show compassion
To all
You have made.
You uphold those
Who fall.
With your hand
You lift up those
Who are bowed down.
With your loving hand
You satisfy the desires
Of every living thing.
As the eyes of all
Look to you,
As they call
On your name
In truth,
You give them
Sustenance in the time
Of their need. Hear my cry,
O Lord. Save me from my
Faithless ways. Only you are
Faithful—all your promises
You keep. All your children
You save. O praise the
Holy name of the
Loving Lord!

Ps. 145:8–9, 13–21

O Lord, truly I am your servant;
 . . . you have freed me from my chains.

I will sacrifice a thank offering to you
 and call on the name of the Lord. [Ps. 116:16–17]

Sacrifice

Because of my disobedience,
Because of my rebellious ways,
I suffered great affliction.
By your hand, Lord,
I was chastened.
Then I called to you
In my trouble,
And in great mercy
You saved me.
You broke away my chains,
The iron chains forged
By my rebellion.
You cut through
The imprisoning bars
And set me free.
Now let me give thanks
To the Lord for
His unfailing love.
Let me bring my offering of
Thanks to you,
An acceptable sacrifice,
The only one you desire—
A spirit truly consecrated
To you, Lord.
May I be conformed no longer
To the pattern of this world.
Transform me, Lord;
Renew my mind.
With my life let me
Worship you. Let me be
A living sacrifice of thanks
To your mercy.

Ps. 107:10–22; 2 Chron. 29, 33; Rom. 12:1–2

May the words of my mouth and the meditation of my heart
    be pleasing in your sight,
    O LORD, my Rock and my Redeemer. [Ps. 19:14]

Pleasing

O Lord, I have brought
To you an offering of
Thanksgiving—a living
Sacrifice, consecrated
To you in worship.
I have dedicated myself
To your holy purpose,
The only pleasing gift
I can give.
Now work out
Your purpose in me—
That which will be
Pleasing to you—
Through the name
Of my Redeemer
And to his glory.

For your kingdom
Is served by the Spirit
Of righteousness,
Peace, and joy
Manifest in the lives
Of those who have given
Themselves to you.
May the meditation
Of my heart be guided
By your Spirit.
May the words
Of my mouth be
An expression of your
Peace and joy.
May my life always be
Pleasing in your sight.

Rom. 12:1–2; Heb. 13:21; Rom. 14:17–18

We will shout for joy when you are victorious
and will lift up our banners in the name of our God.
[Ps. 20:5a]

Banner

The forces of the evil one
Array themselves
Around us.
As the Lord's anointed,
We are subject to attack
From every side.
Yet we need not fear,
For we are protected by
The name
Of the God of Jacob.
He has raised a Banner,
He has unfurled it
Against the fiery arrows
Of the enemy.
Our banner is the Lord!
He will war

Against the foe,
He will win
The victory for us.
With the saving power
Of his right hand,
He will deliver us.
Now let us shout
For joy.
Let us lift up
Our Banner.
We have placed
Our trust in the
Name of the Lord.
In his name
We have been
Saved.

Ps. 20; 60:4; Exod. 17:15

Gladness

O Lord, it is with joy
We come to serve you;
In response to
Your overwhelming love,
We come.
In love we serve
One another,
Knowing that
In truth we serve
The Lord.
Our reward is not
From men, but from
The One whose love
For us endures
Forever. Now let us
Enter your presence

With thanksgiving.
Let us bring to you
Our praise.
For all who seek you
Rejoice, and
All who find you
Are glad.
With shouts of joy
We sing a song
Of praise—praise to the
Name of the Lord!
Your goodness and
Faithfulness are unending.
You have made us for
Your glory, to serve you
With gladness.

Ps. 100; Eph. 6:7–8; Gal. 5:13; Ps. 40:16; 68:3–4

It is he who made us, and we are his. . . . [Ps. 100:3a]

Made

O Lord, by your hand
All things have been
Made. The creation
Is yours, and it is
Good. In such a
Great creation, I am
So small a part,
And yet, with your hands
You shaped me,
You molded me like clay.
With your breath
You gave me life;
With your Spirit
I was formed.
All that I am
Belongs to you,

For you made me
And ordained my days.
O let me praise
You, Lord, for
I am the work
Of your hands, and
All your works
Are wonderful.
O let me learn
To love your
Commands. Give me
Understanding so I
May walk in the
Good and perfect way
You have made
For me.

John 1:3; Gen. 1:31a; Ps. 24:1; Job 10:8–9; 33:4; Ps. 139:13–16;
119:73

Delight yourself in the LORD
and he will give you the desires of your heart. [Ps. 37:4]

Live

Lord, you are the true
Vine—you are the Life!
As I remain in you,
I too have life. I am
Your branch, a living
Part of you.
Through you flows
The enabling Spirit,
Allowing me to bear
Your fruit—true love
Which gives itself for
Others. As I give
Myself to you, as I
Obey your commands,
You fill me with
Your joy. As I keep

Your words within
My heart, you give me
All, and more,
My heart desires.
Lord, may I continue
To live in you,
Rooted firmly,
Growing daily
Stronger by the faith
You have given me.
May the thanksgiving
Of my heart
Overflow in a song
Of praise,
"In him
I live!"

John 15:1–14; Gal. 5:22–25; Col. 2:6

36

He restores my soul. [Ps. 23:3a]

Restores

Lord, as your sheep,
We sometimes stray.
We proudly seek
Our own way, sure we
Can find greener
Pastures on our own.
Separated from
Our Shepherd,
We are vulnerable
To attack.
We are ravaged
By the prowling lion.
But you are the
Good Shepherd;
Not one of your sheep
Is ever lost.
You seek us out,

You bring us home,
Your restore to us
The joy of your
    salvation.
You renew in us
A steadfast spirit.
With thanksgiving
We humble ourselves
Under your mighty hand.
We can give over all
Our worries to you, for
We are under your care.
We can rest
In your provision,
In your grace.
"He restores
My soul."

Ps. 23:1–3a; Isa. 53:6; 1 Peter 5:6–11; Luke 15:4–7; John
    10:27–30; Ps. 51:10, 12

He guides me in paths of righteousness
for his name's sake. [Ps. 23:3b]

Guides

O Lord, you have
Restored to me the joy
Of your salvation.
My rebellious ways
You have not remembered.
According to your great
Mercy and love, you have
Remembered me.
You have restored
My soul.
Now show me
Your ways, O Lord;
Teach me
Your paths.
Guide me in
Your truth,

For you are my
Savior and my
Only hope.
Keep me from straying.
Teach me your ways,
Your loving and
Faithful ways.
In gratitude, I
Humble myself
Under the correction of
Your rod and staff—
From your instruction
I find my comfort.
O guide me with your
Perfect love, and I
Shall never fear.

Ps. 23:3b–4; 25:4–12; 1 John 4:18

You prepare a table before me
  in the presence of my enemies. [Ps. 23:5]

Prepares

O Lord, you have loved me
With an everlasting love.
You have prepared for me
A perfect plan—
Your will
For my life.
I could not know this
On my own, but
As I have responded
To your love
In obedience,
You have revealed,
Through your Spirit,
An understanding of
The magnitude of all
You have freely given
To those who love you.
Through your Spirit,
You teach me
All things;
You guide me into
All truth.
You fill me with
Your presence to
Overflowing. Like streams
Of living water, your Spirit
Flows from me.
Though I am surrounded
By the enemy of my soul,
He cannot stop the flow
From the cup you have
Prepared for me.

· **Eph. 2:10; 1 Cor. 2:9–13; John 14:15–26; 16:13; 7:37–39**

My cup overflows. [Ps. 23:5b]

Overflows

O Lord, you have filled
My cup to overflowing—
With your Spirit
You have filled me.
You have strengthened me
With power through
Your Holy Spirit, that
You may live in me
As I find my life
In you. Through faith
We are one,
Enabling me to know,
At last, the abundance
Of your love.
As I live in you,
I am filled until

I am brimming over
With your love,
With all the fullness
Of you. In every way,
You make your love
Increase and overflow
To those around me.
Your joy and peace
Well up from a heart
That trusts in you—
Through your Spirit
I have been given
The blessed hope,
The assurance that
I will dwell with you
Forever.

Ps. 23:5b–6; John 7:37–39; Eph. 3:16–21; 1:23; Col. 2:6; Rom.
15:13

The LORD is my Shepherd. . . . [Ps. 23:1]

Shepherd

O Lord, my hope is placed
In you. In the strength
Of your arms I rest—
As my Shepherd, you will
Carry me forever.
You bear me up
In a loving embrace,
Your gather me close
To your heart.
Gently you lead the
Sheep of your pasture;
You call us by name
And we come.
For you have brought
Life, and as we remain
In your care, we will

Enjoy the abundance
Of your provision.
You are the Good Shepherd,
And we are your sheep.
You know us, and
We know you in the
Most intimate sense,
For we are one. Therefore,
You have called us to be
Little shepherds,
To willingly care for
Your flock,
To share in your glory
As one who serves,
To love one another as
You have loved us.

Ps. 28:9; Isa. 40:11; John 10:1–18; 1 Peter 5:1–4; John 15:12

Lamb

O Lord, you have entrusted
To us the care and feeding
Of your sheep. You have
Asked us to serve as an
Example to your flock.
As we follow you,
We learn to lead.
And as we serve,
So shall we share
In the glory
Which will be revealed.
We will receive from
Our chief Shepherd the
Crown of everlasting glory.
At that day, we will see
Our Shepherd who was

Made to be a Lamb, slain
For the sin of the world.
We will sing a new song
To you, the Lamb who
Purchased us with his blood—
"Worthy is the Lamb!"
All creation will sing,
"All praise and honor,
Glory and power be to
The Lamb who sits on
The throne." And the Lamb
Will be our Shepherd.
You will lead us to
The living water,
And we will rest
In you forever.

1 Peter 5:1a–4; John 1:29; Rev. 5:9–14; 7:17

Part 2

Ascribe to Him the Glory Due His Name

Ascribe to the LORD the glory due his name;
worship the LORD in the splendor of his holiness. [Ps. 29:2]

Glory

All glory and strength
Belong to the Lord.
Ascribe to him the glory
Due his name.
The Lord is enthroned
Over all he has made.
From his sanctuary comes
The voice of the Lord.
His voice is heard
Over all the earth.
How majestic is
The speech of the Lord—
His words strike fire
Like the flash of lightning.
How powerful is

The shout of the Lord—
His cry is like the mighty
Sound of thunder rolling
Across the waters.
The sound of his glory
Shakes the earth until
All fall before him
And worship the Lord
In the splendor
Of his holiness.
The Lord is in
His holy temple.
At the sound of
His voice, all cry,
"Glory!"

Ps. 29

Sing to the LORD a new song;
sing to the LORD, all the earth. [Ps. 96:1]

Sing

Now bring an offering
To the Lord. Sing
A new song,
All the earth. Come
Into his courts
With praise.
Strength and glory
Are in his sanctuary.
Splendor and majesty
Are ever before him.
O worship the Lord;
He is worthy
Of all praise.
Come sing to the Lord,
All of creation!
Let the heavens

Rejoice,
Let the earth
Be glad,
Let the sea
Resound
With a song
Of jubilation!
Let the creatures
Of the field dance
For joy,
Let the inhabitants
Of the forest sing
Before the Lord.
Let us proclaim his glory
To all nations: "Rejoice, for
The Lord reigns!"

Ps. 96

Let them sing before the LORD,
for he comes to judge the earth. [Ps. 98:9a]

Anticipation

Come, let us rejoice,
For the Lord has done
Marvelous things.
His righteousness has been
Revealed—the ends of the
 earth
Have seen his salvation.
All the earth awaits
Its redemption
At the hand of the Lord.
By his strong right hand
He brings salvation
To his children.
To his creation
Will come liberation and
Our own glorious freedom.
With eager expectation

All the earth awaits
The day of the Lord.
With shouts of joy
And jubilant song
The creation makes
Music to the Lord.
The mountains sing
Together, and
The rivers clap their hands.
All that he has made
 joins
In a song of praise,
For the King is coming!
He will make right all
That has been wrong.
With joyful anticipation
We sing, "Come quickly!"

Ps. 98; Rom. 8:18–21

> For God is the King of all the earth;
>   sing to him a psalm of praise. [Ps. 47:7]

King

Mighty is the King
Who comes. He loves
Justice; he has established
Equity among the peoples.
He has revealed his
    righteousness
To the nations. Let them
    tremble
Before the Lord who reigns.
Great is the Lord
Our God. He is exalted
Over all nations.
Come all peoples
Of the earth, and
Worship at his footstool,
For the Lord our God
Is holy, and worthy
To be praised. He is King

Over all the earth.
O sing to him
A psalm of praise!
Clap your hands,
All tribes and peoples;
Shout aloud with
Cries of joy, for you
Are ruled by the One
Who brings truth and justice.
Great is the King who reigns
Over all the nations—
The kings of the earth
    belong
To him. And to those whom
He has chosen, whom
He loves, belongs the
    inheritance,
The kingdom everlasting.

Ps. 98:2–9; 99:1–5; 47

Blessed is the nation whose God is the LORD,
the people he chose for his inheritance. [Ps. 33:12]

Chosen

O sing a new song
To the Lord, an anthem
Of praise to our God, for
We are his chosen people!
He has called us out
Of darkness and into
His wonderful light.
In great mercy
He has called us,
That we may declare
Praises to the Lord.
He has made us
A royal priesthood,
A holy nation,
A people belonging
To him. Let us,

The righteous of the Lord,
Be music
To his ear. Let us
Come before him
With thanksgiving.
Let us extol him with
A melody of praise,
For our Lord is
The great King.
Let us bow down
In worship—
He is the rock
Of our salvation, and
We are his people,
Chosen to be his
Treasured possession.

1 Peter 2:9–10; Ps. 33:1; 95:1–2, 6–7; 135:4

He provided redemption for his people;
he ordained his covenant forever—
holy and awesome is his name. [Ps. 111:9]

Covenant

May the chosen of the Lord
Praise his holy name!
Great are his works,
Glorious are his deeds
On our behalf.
Let us not forget
The wonder of his
Grace and compassion
Toward us.
At the hand of the Lord
We have received his
Covenant of promise.
He has kept his word
To us. His works
Are faithful and just;
His decree will he keep
For ever and ever.

Holy, holy is the name
Of the Lord. He has
    ordained
His eternal covenant—
We are his people and
He has redeemed us.
From everlasting to
Everlasting, the Lord's love
Is with those who
Revere him. The fear
Of the Lord is the
Beginning of wisdom.
Keep his covenant,
Remember to obey him,
For his righteousness is ours,
His eternal covenant is
    unbroken.

Ps. 111; 103:17–18; Heb. 13:20

For he remembered his holy promise. . . .
He brought out his people with rejoicing,
    his chosen ones with shouts of joy;
he gave them the lands of the nations,
    and they fell heir to what others had toiled for—
that they might keep his precepts
    and observe his laws.

Praise the LORD. [Ps. 105:42–45]

Remembers

The eternal covenant of
    promise
Has been sealed with
    the
Blood of the Lamb.
God has made peace
For us through the
Resurrection of the One
Who was slain.
He will not forget
His holy promise
Secured with such a
Precious bond.
The Lord will redeem
His people from the
Land of death.
He will bring us out

With rejoicing into
New life.
He will deliver
His chosen ones
With shouts of joy.
The Lord will give us
Our inheritance, the
Land of abundance.
He will equip us
With everything good,
Enabling us to
Do his will, to
Keep his precepts.
O praise the eternal
Name of the Lord,
For he remembers
His promise.

Heb. 13:20; Rev. 5:9; 2 Peter 1:2–3

You have laid down precepts
  that are to be fully obeyed.
Oh, that my ways were steadfast
  in obeying your decrees! [Ps. 119:4–5]

Precepts

O Lord, you have kept
Your covenant.
You have remembered
Your holy promise
To us, your chosen people.
You have been faithful
And steadfast in all
You have done
Toward us. Now,
Let us be faithful
To you. Lord,
You have demonstrated
Your great love and care
For us by sharing
Your infinite wisdom.
You have laid down
Your precepts for us
As a right path—
As we follow your way,
You bring joy
To our hearts.
O Lord, keep my feet
Upon the path
Of your commands.
May I be steadfast
In obeying your decrees.
Let me find in your way
My one true delight.
Teach me, O Lord,
To follow your precepts,
That I may grow in my
Understanding of your grace.

Ps. 105:3–4; 19:8; 119:32; 111:10

Give me understanding, and I will keep your law
and obey it with all my heart. [Ps. 119:34]

Understanding

O Lord, you know how foolish
I can be, how easily
I can turn from you
To selfish ambition,
To seeking my own way.
Turn me, now, from
My worthless pursuits.
Turn my eyes to you—
Renew my life
By the power of
Your Word. Teach me,
O Lord, to follow
Your decrees. Guide me
In the path of
Your commands. Give me
A true understanding
Of your will,
That I may obey
You wholeheartedly.
As I diligently study
Your Word, give me
More than knowledge.
Grant me depth of insight—
Enable me to discern
Your truth. Fill me
With your righteousness
So all may see
Your life being
Lived out in me.
May all that I do
Bring glory and praise
To you.

Ps. 119:33–40; Phil. 1:9–11

The fear of the LORD is the beginning of wisdom;
    all who follow his precepts have good understanding.
    To him belongs eternal praise. [Ps. 111:10]

Wisdom

Lord, enable me to accept
Your Word as the one true
Guide for my life.
Turn my ear from
The clamor of the world
To your still small voice—
Speak to my heart.
Help me to seek after
Knowledge of you
As one would search
For precious treasure,
For you are the eternal God
In whom rests all wisdom.
Teach me to come with awe
To the revelation of your Word.
May I come to you with
    reverence.

Help me to see you
As you are,
Majestic in your holiness,
Wise beyond all understanding.
Confer on me this knowledge,
    Lord.
Bestow on me the
Wisdom of your Word.
Then I will have good
Understanding of the path
You have laid out for me—
The way which is right
And just and fair.
O may your mind
Be my own, Lord.
May your wisdom
Be in my heart.

Prov. 2:1–11

Who, then, is the man that fears the LORD?
He will instruct him in the way chosen for him. [Ps. 25:12]

Instruct

I come to you, Lord, with
Thanksgiving and praise,
For you have heard my
    request,
You have answered my
    prayer.
As I reverence your Word,
You have spoken to me
From your revelation.
As I diligently study,
You have faithfully instructed
Me in the way I should go.
You have confided in me
The deep secrets
Of your wisdom.
You have made known to me
The full promise
Of your covenant.

You have taken me
From the place of beginning—
The fear of the Lord—
Along the path you
Have chosen for me.
You have disciplined
My mind so that
I might attain wisdom.
You have given me
An understanding of your
    Word,
Providing me with insight
And discernment.
It is with wonder and awe
That I see your mighty hand
Leading me with love, as a
    father
Instructs his child.

Ps. 25:10, 14; Prov. 1:1–7

Blessed are those . . .
   who walk in the light of your presence, O LORD. [Ps. 89:15]

Walk

Lord, it is with love
That you lead me—
You teach me your way
So I may walk
In your truth.
How blessed am I
To be able to walk
In the way of the Lord.
And yet, there are times
When I choose
To leave the path
Of your instruction.
There are times
When I do not wish
To obey your commands.
I turn from

Your loving presence,
I turn from the Light
And stumble off into
The darkness of
My own sinful desires.
Bereft of your illumination,
I know nothing,
I understand nothing,
I am alone.
But oh, when I walk
With you, when the
Fellowship is restored,
What a joy it is to see,
In the light of your Life,
That I remain purified
By your grace and forgiveness.

Ps. 86:11; 82:5; 1 John 1:5–7

Cleanse me . . . and I will be clean;
    wash me, and I will be whiter than snow. [Ps. 51:7]

Cleansed

O Lord, with your shed blood
I have been forgiven.
By the sprinkling
Of your blood
I have been cleansed.
You have washed
My entire being
With your purity;
You have made me holy
Once for all
Through your sacrifice.
Never again
Will you be made
An offering for sin.
Never again
Will you be slain,

For your blood was
Sufficient; I am now
Pure and blameless
Before you—
Whiter than snow.
O what a wonder
That I have been made
Forever perfect by
Your one sacrifice.
What a marvel is your
Grace that, even now,
You are making perfect
My walk, my manner
Of living. Continue your
Work of perfection in me.
Teach me to walk in purity.

Heb. 9:22b; Eph. 5:25b–27; Heb. 10:22; 9:25–28; 10:10–14

It is God who arms me with strength
and makes my way perfect. [Ps. 18:32]

Perfecting

O Lord, I thank you
For your patience,
For your long-suffering
As you bear with my
Many failings.
You are at work
In my life,
Perfecting my walk,
Making my manner of living
A true reflection
Of the spiritual reality—
I am pure and blameless
Before you.
But oh, my walk is
Anything but blameless.
Too often I stray from
The path of your commands,
I stumble off into the
Dark way of transgression.
My feet become mired
In the filth of sin.
How miserable I am,
Cut off from the warmth
Of our fellowship by
My own disobedience.
Then I remember your words:
"I have washed you, made you
Clean. Now wash your feet
By leaving behind
The darkness and
Stepping into the light
With me."

2 Tim. 2:13; Heb. 12:1–2; Eph. 1:4; 1 John 1:5–7; 2:11; John
13:10

How can a young man keep his way pure?
By living according to your word. [Ps. 119:9]

Purify

O Lord, you have promised
To be ever present.
To walk with me,
To live with me,
To be my God. Now
Let me purify myself
From everything that
Contaminates body and soul—
Everything that separates
Me from fellowship
With you. Now
Let me wash my feet
(My comings and goings,
All that I do)
Of the filth
Of willful disobedience.

May I submit myself
To the instruction
Of your Word. Teach me
To resist the tempter
With the protection
Of your Word. Let me
Step again into the
Fellowship of the Light
And receive your
Welcoming embrace.
Keep me from the folly
Of the double-minded.
May my one true desire
Be to walk before you
With clean hands
And a pure heart.

2 Cor. 6:16–17:1; 1 John 1:5–7; John 13:10; James 4:7–8;
Ps. 86:11

Light

O Lord, you are Light;
Without you, I am
Empty darkness, a void
Waiting to be filled.
But you have come—
A beacon in the night,
You have turned my
Darkness into light.
As on the first day
Of creation, you spoke:
"Let light shine
Out of darkness,"
And it was so.
Your illuminating Presence
Came into my life,
Enabling me to see

You, my glorious Lord,
Giving me the eyes of faith
So I might believe
On you as Savior.
O Lord, you have declared it
As your will that no one
Who believes in you
Should stay in darkness.
May the light of your Word
Be ever present with me.
May my understanding grow
As the dawn of the day.
May my joy in you rise
As the morning star,
The single, incandescent
Focus of my heart.

1 John 1:5; John 1:5a; Ps. 118:27a; 2 Cor. 4:6; John 12:46;
2 Peter 1:19

> Your word is a lamp to my feet
> and a light for my path. [Ps. 119:105]

Illuminate

O Lord, you are Light;
In your presence, I see
Clearly. Your Truth
Guides me in the way
I should go. Your Word
Is the lamp which
Illuminates
My path. Your Life
Is the shining
Example for me
To follow. Your Presence
Fills me with joy,
With unending pleasure,
For you lead me
By the hand,
You reveal to me
The path of life,
The way everlasting.
O Lord, may your
Light and your
Truth always be
My guide. May I
Continue to find
In your presence
My greatest joy
And delight, for
You are the Way,
You are the Truth,
You are the Life.
O Lord, you are the
Light resplendent—
Illuminate me!

Ps. 36:9; 43:3–4; 16:11; John 14:6a

Those who look to him are radiant. . . . [Ps. 34:5a]

Radiant

O Lord, you are Light;
As I follow you, I will
Never walk in darkness—
You will fill me
With your Presence,
With the light of life.
You will make me
A radiant source
Of illumination for
Those lost in darkness,
That they may see you,
Their salvation.
Lord, let my light
So shine that others
Will see in me
Your peace, your hope,
Your joy, your love.
May my life be
Resplendent with the
Beauty of your Presence.
May your righteousness
In me shine
Like the dawn.
Once I belonged to
The night, but now
I belong to you—
I am yours, a
Child of the Light,
And I find, in the
Face of the One I love,
A luminance which
Becomes my own.

John 8:12; 1 Thess. 5:5; Acts 13:47; Matt. 5:14–16; Ps. 37:6

Praise the LORD, O my soul.

O LORD my God, you are very great;
   you are clothed with splendor and majesty. [Ps. 104:1]

Splendor

O Lord, my God, you are
Resplendent with light;
With a garment of light
You array yourself.
You are clothed with
Splendor and majesty.
In majesty you ride forth,
The King victorious,
The Champion of truth
And righteousness.
In your right hand
You hold the scepter
Of justice, the symbol
Of your kingdom.
Your kingdom, O Lord,
Is everlasting. Your

Dominion will endure
For ever and ever.
O let me praise the
Name of the Lord, for
Your name alone
Is exalted; your
Splendor is above the
Earth and heavens!
Let me proclaim
Your glory, so that
All men may know
Of your mighty acts,
Of your awesome deeds.
You are the King of glory!
You are the King of glory!
All praise the King of glory!

Ps. 76:4; 104:2; 45:3–6; 145:11–13; 148:13; 24:10

Praise be to the LORD God, the God of Israel,
who alone does marvelous deeds. [Ps. 72:18]

Marvelous

O shout with joy
To the Lord, our God,
Sing to the glory
Of his name.
Praise him with
Offerings of thanksgiving,
For great are his deeds
On our behalf.
Great and marvelous
Are his deeds,
Just and true
Are his ways—
His righteous acts
Have been revealed.
We come before him
In reverence to worship.
"Only you are holy,

Only you are worthy
Of our praise and
Adoration, for you are
Creator, Savior,
Healer, Redeemer,
Counselor, Restorer,
Refiner, Messiah.
All that you are is
A revelation of
All that you are doing,
All you have accomplished
For our benefit and
To your glory." Let us
   praise
His wonderful name forever,
Let us sing of his marvelous
   deeds.

Ps. 66:1–3; Rev. 15:3–4; Ps. 72:19

Let them praise the name of the LORD,
for he commanded and they were created. [Ps. 148:5]

Creator

The heavens declare your glory,
O Lord; the skies proclaim
The work of your hands.
Day after day they sing
Praise to your name.
The sun, moon, and stars
Praise you, O Maker, for you
Set them in the sky to
Govern day and night.
You set them in place
For ever and ever, and they
Will never pass away.
The chorus of creation is
  joined
By all the creatures of the
  earth.
The great waters echo with
The song of the whale.
The dolphins leap for joy.
The birds fill the dawn
With a madrigal of praise.
Every living thing rejoices
In you, for by your word
They were created. All
You have made sings
Praises to your name.
O may your children join the
Canon of rejoicing, for
Like the stars you have
Made us to shine. You have
Placed us in this world
To proclaim you, the
Word of life, the
Creator of all.

Ps. 148; 19:1–2; Gen. 1:17; Ps. 104:12, 21; Phil. 2:15a, 16b

When we were overwhelmed by sins,
   you atoned for our transgressions.
You answer us with awesome deeds of righteousness,
   O God our Savior,
the hope of all the ends of the earth. . . . [Ps. 65:3, 5]

Savior

The Lord lives! All praise
Be to my Rock and
My Salvation!
My hope is in the
Living God, the One who
Came to save. In him
The grace of God appeared,
Bringing salvation
To all who believe.
He came in kindness and
   love—
Because of his great mercy,
He saved me. Though I was
Covered in the filth of sin,
He took hold of me,
He saved me through
The washing of rebirth and

The renewing of
His Holy Spirit. How generously
He poured out himself
For me, so that
I might be justified
By his grace, so that
I might inherit the
Hope of eternal life.
All praise be to the
Savior who gave himself
For me. All praise be to
My blessed Hope, the
Living Rock of all the ages.
To you, my Savior,
I will sing eternal praises,
For you have saved me by your
   grace.

I said, "O Lord, have mercy on me;
    heal me, for I have sinned against you." [Ps. 41:4]

Healer

There was a time when
I hated you, Lord, when
My heart was filled with
Rebellion against you.
How wretched was my
Existence apart from you,
How miserable my
Sin-sick soul.
Then I called to you
In my distress, and
You came to me as
The living Word,
The Word that heals.
You forgave all my sins,
You healed all my diseases,
But oh, at what a cost!

For you healed me by
Taking upon yourself
My infirmities;
You gave me joy by
Assuming the burden of
My sorrow;
You brought me peace by
Suffering for me
My punishment.
You bore in your own body
The death-bringing sickness
Of my sin. You died
That I might live a life
Of righteousness in you.
Through your suffering, O Lord,
I have been healed.

Ps. 107:17–20; 103:3–4; Matt. 8:16; Isa. 53:4–6; 1 Peter 2:24

O Israel, put your hope in the LORD,
for with the LORD is unfailing love
and with him is full redemption. [Ps. 130:7–8]

Redeemer

May we never forget, Lord,
That once we toiled under the
Whip of the oppressor,
That once we were slaves to
    sin.
We lived without hope,
For we possessed nothing
With which we could
Purchase our freedom.
But praise be to God!
For you came to us.
Because of your unfailing love,
You came to buy us back
From the enemy.
You redeemed us,
Not with silver and gold,
But with your precious blood,

With the blood of
God's perfect Lamb
You bought us.
You brought us up
Out of the land of death,
You lifted us out of the pit.
You exchanged our chains
For crowns of joy—
Because of your great
Love and compassion
You saved us.
O Lord, may we never forget
That we are twice yours,
Yours because you made us,
Yours because you redeemed
    us
With your life.

Rom. 6:17–18; Ps. 106:10; 78:42; 1 Peter 1:18; Ps. 103:4;
    Eph. 1:7

I will praise the LORD, who counsels me. . . . [Ps. 16:7a]

Counselor

I will praise you, Lord,
The all-knowing One,
For by your grace
You stoop low, in love,
To instruct me.
You take me by the hand
And with your counsel
You guide me.
You bring to me,
In yourself,
All that is truth,
Wisdom, and
Understanding.
With all my heart
I will trust in you—
How foolish to depend
On my weak understanding

When I can lean on you.
O Lord, you are all
I need to know!
May your Spirit of counsel
Abide with me always.
Then, by your Spirit,
I will walk in wisdom
And understanding, in the
Power of your good counsel.
As you show me your way,
I will delight in it.
As you reveal yourself to me,
I will reverence you, my Lord.
For you are the Wonderful
    Counselor,
The One who leads me in
    love.

Ps. 18:35b; 73:23b–24a; Prov. 3:5–6; John 14:26; Isa. 11:2–3;
  9:6

Restore us, O LORD God Almighty;
make your face shine upon us,
that we may be saved. [Ps. 80:19]

Restorer

O Lord, in love
You chastise your children,
You discipline us as we
    deserve.
Because of our great sin,
Because of our wrongdoing
You punish us.
You turn your face from us
And allow sin to inflict
Its incurable wound,
Injury beyond healing.
We are left alone,
Without remedy—
We cry out from the pain
That has no cure.
But Lord, in mercy
You forgive your children,
You forgive our iniquity and
Cover all our sins.
Because of your unfailing love
You revive us again.
You turn to us from your
    anger,
Restoring us to health.
You heal our wounds
And bring us comfort.
You turn our mourning
Into song, into a song of
Joy. For you are
The great Restorer,
The One who makes whole
That which sin would destroy.
May I praise you forever,
O Balm of Gilead.

Jer. 30:11; Isa. 57:17, 19; Jer. 30:12–17, 19; Ps. 85:2–7; Jer. 8:22

For you, O God, tested us;
  you refined us like silver. [Ps. 66:10]

Refiner

How easily, Lord, we
Deceive ourselves into
Believing in false gods.
How quickly we
Desert you to
Follow the idols of this world.
With stubborn hearts we
Refuse to acknowledge you,
Happier, for a time, with
Our little gods.
Without your merciful
Intervention, we would
Go on, from one sin
To another, corrupting
Ourselves beyond hope.
In great love, you refine us,

You place us in the
Furnace of affliction.
Through fiery trials
You burn away the dross
Of our stiff-necked pride—
You bring us into the fire
To refine us like silver,
To test us like gold.
You remove from us the
Spirit of impurity.
You banish the names
Of our idols, so that we
Can only call upon the
Name of the one true God,
The Lord who will not yield us,
His glory, to another.

Jer. 9:3, 6–7, 13–14; Isa. 48:4, 10–11

The kings of the earth take their stand
and the rulers gather together
against the LORD
and against his Anointed One. [Ps. 2:2]

Messiah

O Lord, you are the King,
You are the one
Enthroned in heaven,
Supreme, sovereign,
Mighty in power,
And yet—
You sent as
    Father,
You came as
    Son, Messiah, Christ
    The Anointed One.
You came as
    The Way,
    The Gate
Through which
We might enter into
Your righteousness.
You came as
    The Capstone,
    The solid Rock
Of our salvation.

But you were rejected—
The kings and rulers of
This earth conspired
Against you; they plotted
Your death. In vain
They stood against you.
For you are
    The King eternal—
    The One
Who has conquered death!
You will rule the nations
As your inheritance, and
They will serve you
In fear and trembling.
Lord of all the earth,
You came as
    Messiah,
You died as
    Son,
You rule as
    King of glory.

Ps. 2; 118:19–24; John 3:16

72

> Who is he, this King of glory?
>   The LORD Almighty—
>   he is the King of glory. [Ps. 24:10]

Almighty

Who is the King of glory?
He is
    The Lord Creator,
    Maker of heaven and earth.
The earth is his, and all who
    live—
O praise his holy name!
He is
    The Lord our Savior,
    The shining Hope of glory
For all who believe in him.
He is
    The Lord our Healer,
Pierced for our
    transgressions,
Wounded for our healing—
Sing praise to his holy
    name!
He is
    The Lord Redeemer,
    The purchase Price
        of blood—
    The precious Life
        that bought us,

That freed us from our bonds.
He is
    The Lord our Counselor,
    Our Comforter and Guide,
    Truth-teller, Peace-giver,
    The eternal Indweller.
He is
    The Lord Restorer,
    The Balm of Gilead.
He is
    The Lord Refiner,
    The purifying Flame.
O praise
    The Lord Messiah,
    The chosen One who came.
He died to rise in triumph,
The conquering Lord of all.
Who is
    The King of glory?
He is
    The Lord Almighty,
Strong in battle—
He has won
The final victory for us!

Ps. 24:1, 8; Col. 1:27; Isa. 53:5; 1 Peter 1:18; John 14:15, 26–27;
    Jer. 8:22; Isa. 10:17; Rom. 1:3–4

O LORD, our Lord,
   how majestic is your name in all the earth. [Ps. 8:1a]

Majestic

O King of glory,
Almighty Lord,
How majestic is your name!
You reign upon a throne
Established long ago—
You are from all eternity
The sovereign Lord
Most holy.
O King of glory,
Eternal Lord,
How majestic is your name!
You set your glory
Above the heavens, the
Heavens you have made.
You call forth songs of
   praise
From all creation.
O King of glory,

Creation's Lord,
How majestic is your name!
You make for yourself
A garment of majesty—
In splendor you are arrayed.
All glory, glory! be
   ascribed
To your most holy name.
O great is the Lord, and
   worthy—
Most worthy is he of praise.
In praise I will lift high
My hands—in his name
I will rejoice. O Lord,
My Lord, how
   majestic
Is your name
In all the earth!

Ps. 8; 93:1–2; 45:3; 34:3; 96:4; 63:4

Part 3

May the Whole Earth
Be Filled with His Glory

Praise be to his glorious name forever;
may the whole earth be filled with his glory.
Amen and Amen.   [Ps. 72:19]

Filled

O Lord, let me praise
Your glorious name—
Let me praise
Only you, for
You have ascended
In splendor, higher
Than all the heavens,
In order to fill
The universe with
Your Presence.
O Lord of the universe,
You fill everything
In every way.
Now, out of your
Glorious riches, fill me.
Fill me to the measure of
Your immeasurable fullness.
Fill me with your
Fruitful Spirit,
That I may share
The bounty of
Your righteousness,
That I may glorify
You and bring
Praise to your name.
Pour yourself, through me,
Out into a needy world.
Pour yourself until
The whole earth is
Filled with you.
Fill me, O Lord, until
Only your glory is seen.

Ps. 148:13; Eph. 4:10; 1:22–23; Gal. 5:22; Phil. 1:11

May my lips overflow with praise,
for you teach me your decrees. [Ps. 119:171]

Flow

O Lord, you have filled
My heart with yourself,
With your Word
I have been taught.
Your instruction
Pours into me
Day by day and
Floats away the
Cluttered debris of self
Until I am freed
Of all obstructions,
A clean vessel
Through which you
May flow.
From the abundance
Of my heart,

Let me praise you, Lord.
Let me sing of my joy
In your Word.
May my life always be
A clear channel
Through which
Streams of living water
Will flow
Out to those who
Thirst for you.
Teach me to love you
In obedience,
To keep the way open,
So that your Spirit may
Continue to flow
Unhindered.

Luke 6:45; Ps. 119:172; John 7:37–38

Blessed is the man . . .
[whose] delight is in the law of the LORD . . . .
He is like a tree planted by streams of water,
    which yields its fruit in season . . . . [Ps. 1:1–3]

Tree

O Lord, you have planted me
Like a tree in the wasteland,
A tree whose roots reach
Deep down to the hidden
Stream of life. It is
Your Holy Spirit who
Nourishes me through
The Word. I delight in
The sustenance you bring
As your revelation becomes
A part of me, deep within
My soul. From there,
You move unseen,
Through my very being,
Strengthening me with
Your power, filling me with
Your life.
You flow to my every
Extremity, and then you
Burst forth with an
Abundance of fruit.
You cover that part of me
Which reaches out to
The hungry world
With the Fruit of
Righteousness. It is for
Your glory that I bear
Much fruit, for as
Those in need taste of
Your bounty, they see
That you are good,
That only you can satisfy.

John 7:38–39; Gal. 5:22; Phil. 1:11; John 15:8; Ps. 34:8

Blessed is the man . . .
[whose] delight is in the law of the LORD . . . .
He is like a tree planted by streams of water,
    which yields its fruit in season . . . . [Ps. 1:1–3]

Fruitful

I thank you, Lord,
For making me, like
A tree, to be one who
Draws others to the
Abundance you have provided.
It is by the fruit of
Your Spirit that the
Hungry recognize you
In me. It is to you
They come. It is of you
They partake as they enjoy
Your goodness,
Your righteousness,
Your truth.
O Lord, keep me from
The blight of sin,

Keep me from inhibiting
The life-giving flow
Of your Spirit through
Willful disobedience.
You know my weakness—
Oh, be my strength!
Apart from you
I can do nothing.
Apart from you
I will be fruitless,
My life a barren waste.
But in you, I can do
All things! I can be
A fruitful tree,
Resplendent in the
Beauty of your Spirit.

Gen. 2:9; Eph. 5:9; John 15:5, 10; Phil. 4:19

Blessed is the man . . .
[whose] delight is in the law of the LORD . . . .
He is like a tree planted by streams of water,
    which yields its fruit in season . . . . [Ps. 1:1–3]

Fruit

O Lord, I ask you to
Bear much fruit in me,
An abundance of your grace
Which will draw those
Who hunger to you.
May the fruit of
    righteousness
Be found in my life,
Tangible evidence
Of your Holy Spirit.
May those in need reach out
To test the reality of love
Given unconditionally.
May those in pain come
To find your peace.
May the intolerant see
The way of your patience;

May the uncaring be
Moved by your kindness.
May those who do evil
Be surprised at your goodness;
May those who break faith
Be humbled by your
    faithfulness.
May the uncontrollably angry
    receive
A gentle, controlled reply.
May I demonstrate, in every
    way,
Your love which embraces
The unlovely, the unloved.
Let me live in your Spirit.
Let me be sustenance
For those in need of you.

John 15:8; Gal. 5:22–23

Because you are my help,
I sing in the shadow of your wings. [Ps. 63:7]

Shadow

O Lord, I rejoice in you,
For through the times of
Difficulty, you remain
My refuge, my protection.
In the midst of disaster
I can rest securely in
The shadow of your wings.
But oh, there are so many
Who struggle on alone,
Who try to win the fight
In their own strength,
Who are finally overcome
   by the
Futility of their effort, and
   still
Are not willing
To come to you. Still

They resist, they reject
The One who longs to
Gather them under his wings.
O Lord, if only they knew
How you sorrow for those
Outside your care,
How you desire to send
Your love to those
Who call on you.
Lord, may the lost and weary
Believe in the Refuge
Because they see my rest.
May they believe in the Joy
Because they hear my song.
May they believe in you
Because they see around me
The shadow of your wings.

Matt. 23:37; Ps. 57:1–3

I said, "Oh, that I had the wings of a dove!
I would fly away and be at rest. . . ." [Ps. 55:6]

Wings

I asked
For the wings of a dove
To carry me far from
The turmoil of difficulty
Surrounding me, but
I could not escape the
Anguish of my soul.
I cried out
To you, Lord: "Don't you
See, don't you care?
Where are you, Lord?"
Then you
Reminded me: "Don't you
Remember how I delivered
   you
From bondage? Don't you
Remember how I carried you

On eagles' wings and
Brought you to myself?
I am still the Lord,
The everlasting God. I am he
Who does not grow weary,
Who renews the strength of
   those
Whose hope is in the Lord."
Then you
Turned my eyes from
My circumstances to
Yourself. You lifted me
On the wings of hope
And together we soared
Far above and beyond
The receding landscape
Of my limitations.

Ps. 55:3–8; Isa. 40:27; Exod. 19:4–6; Isa. 40:28–31

The Lord upholds all those who fall
and lifts up all who are bowed down. [Ps. 145:14]

Lifts

O Lord, my hope is placed
In you, the One who remains
Forever faithful. You are
My ever-present help
In time of need. You are
The loving Lord who
Lifts me when I fall.
It is to you I call when I
Am bowed down with care.
But what of those who
Do not know your name?
O lift them, Lord,
Through me.
Love them, Lord,
Through me.
Let me be
    compassion
To the oppressed;

Let me be
    sustenance
To those who hunger.
Let me be
    freedom
To those who are bound;
Let me be
    sight
To those who are blind.
Let me be
    Your strong right hand
Which upholds those who are
Cast down.
Let me be
    You,
The One who lifts up.
As you have loved me, so
Let me be.

Ps. 146:5–6; 145:18; 80:18; 146:7–8; John 15:12

I love you, O LORD, my strength. [Ps. 18:1]

Love

O Lord, you are LOVE.
You are love that does not
Grasp life, but
Gives it up—you gave
Yourself for me.
You are love that does not
Cling to self but
Lets it go to lift another.
You would have me love
As you do, but it is not
In me to love my brother—
I love myself too well.
In placing myself first,
I became last, and nearly
Lost until you began to
Show me the way of love.

Through your example, I am
Beginning to understand that
Love is giving up one's self,
Not giving to one's self.
By following you, I am
Learning to give my life
For others, to expend myself
With joy, not counting the cost.
O lead me in the way of love,
Be my strength, be my guide.
Enable me to love you first,
To love you most of all.
May I give myself—
Heart, mind, and soul—to you,
And through you, to others,
A gift of love.

Phil. 2:5–8; John 15:12; Matt. 22:37–38

I love you, O LORD, my strength. [Ps. 18:1]

Offering

O Lord, you are LOVE,
A fragrant offering,
The sweet Sacrifice of self
Which makes love possible
In us. Now help me
To be like you,
To live a life of love,
To give myself to the need
In others. Help me
To see the emptiness,
The brokenness, the loneliness,
To perceive the hidden pain.
May I be willing
To fill by emptying myself,
To heal by being broken.
May I be able

To walk the long, lonely road
With those who live in pain,
To offer myself as
Comfort and companion.
It is easy to love with words,
But you have called me
To love with my life,
To give it up,
To pour it out
For those in need of you.
May I lay down my life
Gladly, knowing I live
In you. May I present myself
A willing sacrifice, an
Aromatic offering
Of love.

Eph. 5:1–2; 1 John 3:16–18

I love you, O LORD, my strength. [Ps. 18:1]

Sincere

O Lord, you are LOVE,
Love which goes beyond
Mere words—you are
Love in action,
Love in truth.
Help me to be,
Like you, the
Sincere expression of
Love which moves
Past the bounds of
Convention to a
True illustration of
Love at work. May I
Devote myself to my
Brother's needs, placing them
Above my own. May I

Bless the one who
Curses me, and live
In harmony with
All around. May I
Rejoice with those who
Celebrate, and
Mourn with those who
Sorrow. May I
Remember, in all I do,
I am serving you, and so be
Joyful in hope,
Patient in affliction,
Faithful in prayer.
May I share you
With those in need,
The true expression of love.

1 John 3:16–18; Rom. 12:9–18

Not to us, O LORD, not to us
but to your name be the glory,
because of your love and faithfulness. [Ps. 115:1]

Faithful

O Lord, you are LOVE,
You are compassion which
Never fails. Because of
Your great love, we receive
Mercy—you continue
To be faithful, even when
We fail you. You keep on
Caring though we become
Careless of our relationship
With you. Through all my
Faithless ways, you have
Remained loving, you have
Remained true. Now teach me
To love as faithfully as you
Love me. May I love with
Patience, willing to wait

For those who need time
To grow. May I love with
Kindness, able to go beyond
The limit of my needs to meet
Another's. May I love with
Gentleness, never urging or
Persuading, but keeping pace
Faithfully, joyfully.
Above all, teach me to love,
Not for the sake of being
Loved by others, but for you,
For your name and
To your glory. May my life
Be a way of simply saying,
"The Lord is faithful;
He is love."

Lam. 3:23; Gal. 5:22–23

For great is his love toward us,
  and the faithfulness of the LORD endures forever.

Praise the LORD. [Ps. 117:2]

Faithfulness

O Lord, you are LOVE,
Love unfailing—
Great is your faithfulness!
Let me sing a
Song of praise to you,
The One whose word
Is true, whose name
Is Faithful. Exalted be
The name of the Lord—
Your love endures forever!
Your infinite love stretches
Beyond my imagination,
Beyond the grasp of my
Understanding. O Lord,
Your love reaches to the
  heavens,
Your faithfulness to the skies.

I see your righteousness
Rising above me like a
Summitless mountain;
I feel your justice
Beneath me as a
Fathomless deep.
All that you are
Surrounds me,
Goes beyond me,
Expanding to fill the universe,
  until
You are all in all.
I will never comprehend
The greatness of your love, but
I can see your faithfulness,
And for me, that is the
Reality of love.

Ps. 138:2; 36:5–6; Eph. 1:23

Blessed is the man you choose
and bring near to live in your courts!
We are filled with the good things of your house,
of your holy temple. [Ps. 65:4]

Courts

It is with songs of joy
That I come before you—
Songs which carry me
Into your presence.
On a canticle of thanksgiving
I enter your gates,
With a hymn of praise
I am conveyed into
Your courts. O Lord,
You are all that is good!
Your love endures forever,
Your faithfulness through
All generations. O praise
The name of the Lord!
Let me proclaim,
"The Lord is righteous!"
Let me remain

Righteous in you.
Do not allow me to
Leave your presence
Through doubt or
disobedience,
But plant me, like a tree,
In the court of the Lord.
May I blossom forth
With fragrant songs
Of praise. May I
Grow and flourish there,
Bearing fruit, sharing
Your goodness with all.
May I remain evergreen,
A paean of praise,
A living tree in the court of the
Lord.

Ps. 100; John 15:4; Ps. 92:12–15; Exod. 15:13, 17

One thing I ask of the LORD . . .
that I may dwell in the house of the LORD
   all the days of my life,
to gaze upon the beauty of the LORD
   and to seek him in his temple. [Ps. 27:4]

Dwell

How lovely is
Your dwelling place, O Lord,
How beautiful your house—
Better one day in the
Court of the Lord than
A thousand anywhere else.
How blessed are those
Who abide with you—
May it ever be true
Of me. May I
Remain in you,
Faithful. May I
Walk in your strength,
Blameless. May I
Never practice the ways
Of deceit—no one who

Speaks from a false heart
May stand
In your presence.
O keep me
From the way of sin,
From disobedience
Which removes me
From the abiding place
Of love. May I live
As an obedient servant
In your house. May I never
Be at home with the wicked.
All the days of my life,
May I dwell at peace
In the sanctuary
Of my Lord.

Ps. 84:10; John 15:4; Ps. 101:6–7

Send forth your light and your truth,
    let them guide me . . .
    to the place where you dwell.
Then will I go to the altar of God,
    to God, my joy and my delight. [Ps. 43:3–4a]

Altar

O Lord, you have sent forth
Your truth as a beacon
To guide me. You have
Brought me to your
Holy mountain, to the
Place where you dwell.
You have created in me
A pure heart; you have
Washed from my hands
The stain of sin.
O may I lift these hands
To you in praise,
For you have made me
Blameless in your sight.
Now, Lord, keep my walk
Blameless; keep me from
The way of sin. May I
Lay my life before you,
Consecrated daily—
Worship in love.
May I give myself
To you, O Lord,
Without hesitation,
With no reservation—
May I find the
Act of sacrifice
My greatest joy,
My heart's delight,
For in giving up myself
I am gaining more of you,
And so I find the altar
A place of true rejoicing.

Ps. 51:10; 24:3–4

But let all who take refuge in you be glad;
    let them ever sing for joy.
Spread your protection over them,
    that those who love your name may rejoice in you.
    [Ps. 5:11]

Rejoice

O Lord, you are my refuge,
You are my hope. In you
I find peace
Beyond understanding. In you
I find shelter
In the midst of the storm.
For you spread your protection
Over me—you are my shield
And my salvation. Now let me
Rejoice in you, let me
Sing praise to your holy name.
Your love is unfailing, O Lord.
I will wait upon you
And be glad, for I know
You see my affliction and
You care for me. Through my

Distress, you are allowing me
To grow in my understanding
Of your goodness. For in the
Midst of my difficulty, you have
Poured out your love. You have
Filled my heart with
Your Presence, with
Your own Holy Spirit—
You have filled me with joy.
O Lord, I can rejoice in
Suffering, because I
Rejoice in the hope that
You will be glorified in
My song. Let me sing now,
At rest in the shelter
Of your wings.

Phil. 4:7; Ps. 33:20–22; Rom. 5:3–5; 1 Peter 4:13

For he has not despised or disdained
the suffering of the afflicted one;
he has not hidden his face from him
but has listened to his cry for help. [Ps. 22:24]

Suffering

O Lord, you have called me
To follow in your steps,
To love as you have loved,
To give as you have given,
To suffer as you have suffered.
You have called me to this
Fellowship, to this
Oneness. O may I rejoice
As I participate in
Your sufferings, for
Through this pain, I am
Being likewise perfected, I am
Being made holy unto you.
O work your skillful purpose
In me. Test me, try me,
Produce in me perseverance
And a hope which clings
To growing faith,
Faith made complete,
Faith proven out,
Faith beyond price—
The crown of life.
May this shining faith
Adorn my life, an
Ornamentation of praise
To you, O Lord. May your
Glory be revealed, may your
Faithfulness be seen by all.
For you have called me beyond
Suffering to triumph, beyond
The pain of this moment
To your eternal glory.

1 Peter 2:21; Phil. 3:10; 1 Peter 4:12–13; Heb. 2:10–11; James
1:2–4, 12; Rom. 5:3–5; 1 Peter 5:10

Glorify the LORD with me;
      let us exalt his name together. [Ps. 34:3]

Glorify

O Lord, I will praise you,
I will glorify your name.
With all my heart I will
Praise you, for you are the
Faithful Creator, the
Loving Lord. You have
Made me—I am yours,
Now use me as you will.
If in your service I have
Cause to suffer, let me
Praise you still. Let me
Continue, with joy, to do
The work you have given me,
For then I will bring
Glory to your name.
May I ever sing of you,
For in your love I have
More than life itself.
In your love I have Life
Which goes beyond the
Limitations of the moment,
Which transcends concerns
For health, wealth, or
      security.
In you, I have an abundance
Of grace and peace, I have
All I need. May I lift
These hands, emptied of
      everything
But praise for you. May I
Lift them high to glorify
Your name. May my song
Move others to say, "Come,
Let us glorify the Lord!"

Ps. 86:12; 1 Peter 4:19; John 17:4; Ps. 63:3–4; 2 Peter 1:2–3

Be exalted, O God, above the heavens;
let your glory be over all the earth. [Ps. 57:11]

Exaltation

Come, let us
Glorify the Lord, let us
Exalt his name together.
Let us join in an anthem
Of praise to the Lord—
May we be songs of joy
Heard over all the earth.
Let us clasp hands in a
Dance of rejoicing—
May we be jubilation
Seen by all peoples.
Come, let us sing,
Let us dance together—
We will be a celebration
To the Lord!
We will tell
Of his loving faithfulness,
Of his great faithfulness
Toward us.
We will proclaim
Him to the nations,
We will extol
His holy name.
We will exalt
The Lord, our God, with
The praise of our lives;
We will lift
His name above us with
Our song. We will be
Exaltation, we will be a
Demonstration of his
Glory, seen by all.

Ps. 34:3